holiday *Eggs*

holiday *Eggs*

written by

GEORGEANNE BRENNAN

conceived & produced by

JENNIFER BARRY DESIGN

photography by

RICHARD G. JUNG

10

TEN SPEED PRESS
BERKELEY · TORONTO

Ten Speed Press
Box 7123
Berkeley, California 94707
www.tenspeed.com

Distributed in Australia by Simon & Schuster Australia, in Canada by Ten Speed Press Canada,
in New Zealand by Southern Publishers Group, in South Africa by Real Books, in Southeast Asia by Berkeley Books,
and in the United Kingdom and Europe by Airlift Book Company.

Conceived and Produced by Jennifer Barry Design, Sausalito, California
Design Assistant: Leslie Barry
Layout Production: Kristen Wurz
Copy Editor: Carolyn Miller
Food Stylist: Amy Nathan
Prop Stylist: Carol Hacker / Tableprop, San Francisco
Craft and Floral Stylist: Sarah Dawson
Proofreading: Barbara King

Library of Congress Cataloging-in-Publication Data on file with publisher.
ISBN 1-58008-399-4

Printed in Hong Kong

1 2 3 4 5 6 7 8 9 10 — 06 05 04 03 02

Acknowledgments

Georgeanne Brennan would like to thank the following people:
My husband, Jim Schrupp, for his enthusiastic recipe testing and sampling and astute editing.
My children, Ethel, Oliver, Tom, and Dan, and their friends, all of whom
have sampled and critiqued my egg dishes over the years. Jennifer Barry for asking me
to participate in this project and for allowing me to be part of yet another
of her many beautiful books. Charlotte Kimball, Tom Neely, and Tom Olson for their
thoughtful recipe testing and opinions. Carolyn Miller for her diligent editing. Amy Nathan
for her inspired styling, and Richard Jung for the beautiful photography.

Jennifer Barry Design and the photography and styling team would like
to thank and acknowledge the following individuals for their help on this book project:
Marta Hallett and Gabrielle Pecarsky for their enthusiastic support and guidance;
photography assistant Ivy and styling assistant Nan Golding for their help in creating
the photography and recipes; Jane Bay for her hospitality and use of her home for our photography
location; Yankee Girl and Legacy Antiques, San Anselmo; Alan of Nozaki Enterprises,
San Francisco; Tom Johnson for production assistance; Maria Hjelm for marketing support;
Blake Hallanan and Caroline Hallanan Doyle for their modeling assistance;
and Maria, Ted, Jacob and Evie Michon for loaning us their beautiful *pysanky*.

Introduction

Throughout history and across cultures, eggs have been one of humankind's most basic foods and most potent symbols. Eggs from the nests of wild birds supplied early hunters and gatherers, and from the earliest dawn of agriculture birds were kept in captivity to provide a steady supply of eggs for food. Today, eggs are essential in making a wide variety of dishes, from desserts to omelettes. They are beaten and folded into cakes and soufflés to lighten them, and beaten with milk and seasonings, both sweet and savory, to produce firm, silky custards. Eggs are used to make breads, pastries, and cookies, to create sauces and drinks, and to make glazes. Soufflés and meringues are made almost entirely of egg whites beaten to frothy peaks, while whole eggs are beaten to make frittatas and omelettes, and can be fried, baked, boiled, poached, and roasted.

Eggs have long been associated with fertility and the coming of spring. Because most birds begin to lay eggs as the days lengthen in spring, the egg became symbolic of the season of rebirth, of celebration, and of thanks for the renewal of life. With all our conveniences today, it is almost impossible for us to imagine the life of our ancestors, who depended critically on nature and the seasons, and to understand the hope and anticipation with which they annually awaited the warming of the earth when the world around them came to life again.

Lacquered eggs were given as springtime gifts in ancient China, while in pagan England, red eggs were said to honor Thor and those painted yellow honored the goddess of light. Legend and superstition surrounded eggs. All eggshells had to be burned and thoroughly destroyed, for example, because witches, who were unable to cross water, could use even a tiny piece of shell as a boat. Ancient Greek and Roman cultures also valued eggs. They were exchanged between friends as gifts and even buried in tombs. The Jewish Passover seder includes hardboiled eggs to dip into salted water, the eggs symbolizing rebirth, the salted water bitter tears. With the advent of Christianity, the egg became the symbol of the resurrection of Christ, and in many cultures, traditional decorated eggs associated with spring became linked to Easter.

Ukrainian eggs, also called *pysanky*, are among the most elaborate of the decorated eggs, and versions of them are made throughout Eastern Europe. Shells of raw eggs are traditionally decorated using a wax-resist technique, like that of batik, to create complex, multicolored designs covering the entire egg. Adorned with symbols of the earth, such as wheat for a good harvest or chickens for fertility, and religious or geometric and floral designs, Ukrainian eggs are small pieces of art. On Easter, they are taken to church to be blessed as part of the traditional basket, which also includes a special Easter bread, sausage, cheese, butter, and solid-colored hard-boiled eggs.

Other cultures use decorated eggs at Easter for games. *Cascarones*, which are blown eggs filled with confetti and decorated with paint and paper, are a Mexican tradition. Today, children break them over each other's heads during party games, and children and adults alike use them during fiestas and at carnival, the feasting and celebratory period before Lent. In the late nineteenth and early twentieth century, *cascarones* were part of the courtship ritual, when young men and women broke them over each other's heads in flirtation.

In the United States, children are equipped with baskets and sent out on an Easter egg hunt to find the colorful dyed or painted eggs hidden for them by the Easter Bunny. The tradition of dyeing eggs for Easter is said to have come to the United States with early German immigrants. Danish children roll dyed eggs down hills to see whose egg can make it down without breaking, and the winner takes all the eggs. Egg rolling is also popular in England, and was first introduced to the White House in the early 1800s by Dolly Madison. Egg rolling on the White House lawn is still an Eastertime tradition.

Types of Eggs

Domesticated chickens are the predominant egg layers around the world, although other domesticated birds, such as duck, goose, and quail, are popular too. Chicken eggs are by far the most common in Western cultures. There are many breeds of chickens, and it is the breed that determines whether the eggs are white or brown. Chickens with white feathers and white earlobes lay white eggs, and those with red feathers and red earlobes lay brown. In the United States, the cultural preference is for white eggs, while in Europe brown eggs are preferred. The Arucana is a small breed of chicken whose hens lay eggs with shells in varying hues of pastel blue and aquamarine, looking like already-colored Easter eggs. There is no discernable flavor difference among chicken eggs with different-colored shells.

Duck and goose eggs are larger than chicken eggs and have a slightly stronger, more intense egg flavor. Quail eggs are quite small, no larger than the tip of your thumb. Their shells are a light tan, beautifully speckled with brown, and the eggs are similar in flavor to chicken eggs.

Freshness, Size, and Quality

Newly laid eggs have a rich, intense taste. The thick white clings closely to the round, ball-like yolk, making them excellent for poaching and frying. After about forty-eight hours, the egg white begins to thin and the yolk to flatten, and the flavor becomes less rich and intense, although eggs can safely be refrigerated at home for up to three weeks.

The color of the yolk depends on the diet of the bird. Most commercially raised chickens produce eggs with yolks of a medium yellow. Deep-golden yolks are often the hallmark of eggs from small farmers whose flocks have been allowed to forage or otherwise eat a lot of green plants.

Eggs are sized according to weight per dozen. Jumbo eggs are the largest, followed by extra large, large, medium, and small. Eggs are graded AA, A, or B. The AA have a thicker white and a rounder, fuller yolk, and the egg is more compact. Those labeled A have a thinner white and a slightly flatter yolk. The B grade is rarely seen in retail markets.

Egg Properties

Eggs are invaluable in cooking because of their reaction with other ingredients and for the variety of ways in which they can be used. Whole eggs and egg whites, when beaten, trap air and can be used to produce light cakes and breads, omelettes, and soufflés. If overbeaten, however, the whites will break down and separate. Beaten at room temperature, egg whites will produce a greater volume, although current safety concerns discourage leaving uncooked eggs unrefrigerated.

Egg yolks have an emulsifying property. The lecithin and the cholesterol in the yolk allow a sauce to be thickened with a fat, rather than with a starch such as flour. This characteristic is the principle behind vinaigrettes, mayonnaise, and smooth, silky hollandaise and béarnaise sauces.

In France, egg whites are traditionally beaten in unlined copper bowls as a chemical reaction between the egg whites and the copper makes the egg foam stronger and more resistant to overbeating. In lieu of a copper bowl, cream of tartar strengthens the foam in similar ways.

The addition of other ingredients also affects the cooking of an egg. Adding liquid or sugar will slow the cooking time for eggs, whereas adding salt or an acidic ingredient like lemon juice will speed up the cooking time.

Cracking, Separating, and Beating Eggs

To crack an egg, tap its middle sharply on the edge of a bowl. A metal bowl with a thin edge will give the cleanest break. Using your thumbs and fingers, pull the halves of the shell apart and let the egg fall into the bowl.

To separate the white from the yolk, have two clean, dry bowls ready. If the whites are going to be beaten, their bowl should be large enough to allow the incorporation of air. Crack the egg as directed, and as you pull the shells apart, let the bulk of the white fall into the large bowl, capturing the yolk in one of the egg shell halves. Drop the yolk into the other shell half, letting more of the remaining white fall out. Repeat until only the yolk remains. Drop it into the other bowl.

If the yolk breaks while you are separating the white, quickly move it away from the whites, as any yolk mixed into egg whites will decrease their ability to reach their maximum volume when beaten. Use a moist paper towel or a bit of eggshell to remove any bits of yolk from the white. To beat egg whites, use an electric mixer or a large balloon whisk.

Egg Storage and Safety

Store eggs in the refrigerator after purchase. Eggs in any form, cooked or raw, should be kept refrigerated until ready to use. Although egg whites will develop more volume if they are at room temperature when beaten, it is not necessary, and current health concerns discourage the practice.

Boiling Eggs

Whole boiled eggs are usually eaten at one of three stages: soft-boiled, medium-boiled, and hard-boiled. Soft-boiled eggs have a liquid yolk and a soft white, medium-boiled a soft yolk and a firm white, and hard-boiled eggs are firm throughout.

To discourage cracking while cooking, place cold eggs in cold water and bring just to a boil. Remove the pan from the heat and let stand for 4 to 5 minutes for soft-boiled, 6 to 7 minutes for medium-boiled, and 15 minutes for hard-boiled. Remove from the water and run cold water over the eggs to stop further cooking. This method produces the most tender whites and yolks.

Alternatively, put eggs into cold water and bring to a boil over medium heat. Reduce the heat to medium and cook in gently boiling water for 3, 5 to 7, or 12 to 15 minutes respectively. Run cold water over the eggs to stop the cooking.

Poaching Eggs

Poached eggs are cooked in simmering water until the white is firmly set but the yolk is still soft. They may be eaten on their own; served on toast or muffins either with or without a sauce, as in Eggs Benedict (page 23); or used to top vegetables, meat, or salads, as in Frisée Salad with Poached Egg (page 16). If possible, use AA eggs for poaching because they will make a more compact cooked egg.

To poach eggs, put at least 2 inches of unsalted water in a skillet or other shallow pan. Bring the water to a simmer just below a boil, then break the egg into a saucer or shallow bowl and gently slide the egg into the water. If you are poaching more than one egg, leave about 1 inch between them. Reduce heat to very low and simmer for 4 to 5 minutes, depending on the desired firmness. Remove each egg to a plate using a slotted spoon in the order they were added to the pan. Trim the ragged edges with kitchen scissors or a knife.

Scrambling Eggs

For scrambled eggs, the eggs are broken into a bowl, beaten together, and cooked over low heat to form curds. The curds may be large or small, creamy, soft, or firm, depending on personal taste and the method of cooking. They can be cooked in a skillet or over simmering water in a double boiler. If stirred constantly during the cooking, the curds will be very fine. Intermittent stirring or scraping with the back of a pancake turner will allow larger curds to develop and set. The addition of butter or cream will produce richer eggs, but water or milk will thin them. Other additional ingredients, such as herbs, bits of cheese, or minced green onion may be added during the cooking or toward the end.

Omelettes

Omelettes, though also made from beaten eggs, are cooked undisturbed over medium-high heat until the underside becomes firm but the upper portion is still soft and creamy. The degree of softness depends on personal taste and the method of cooking. Omelettes can be folded to finish cooking their uppermost layer, left flat and turned over like a pancake to cook the other side, or left upright and slipped under a broiler.

Classic omelettes are folded in half or in thirds, either left plain or with fillings to finish cooking. Flat omelettes, which usually contain a considerable amount of flavoring, like spinach, artichokes, or shellfish, are either flipped, pancake style, or finished under a broiler.

Decorating with Eggs

Whole eggshells, eggshell halves, and hard-boiled eggs can be used to make springtime decorations. Some, like the Ukrainian eggs (page 97), come from long traditions and celebrate a specific holiday, while others, like spring napkin rings (page 32) are contemporary and suitable to any occasion.

Raw eggs are used to make the traditional Ukrainian-style decorated eggs. These eggs are *never* eaten.

To hard-boil eggs for decorating, follow the instructions on page 11 (Boiling Eggs). Let stand in cold water to stop the cooking. Remove and let dry before beginning any dyeing or decorating. An egg carton makes a good drying rack.

To Make Hollow Eggs

Wash and dry a raw egg. Prick one end with a pin, piercing the shell and membrane. Pierce the other end, but make the hole larger. To do this, move the pin in a circular motion to wear down the shell. A bit of the shell may break off, but this is fine, as it will make a slightly larger hole.

Holding the egg carefully in one hand over a bowl, fit your lips tightly over the small hole and blow as hard as you can. The bulk of the white first, then later the yolk and the remaining white, will be blown out of the larger hole and into the bowl. This may take 5 or even 10 minutes to accomplish, depending on the force of your breath. Once the eggshell is empty, carefully wash off any bits of egg and set the shell aside to dry before decorating it.

Cracking Eggs for Decorative Shell Halves

If you want eggshell halves with attractive, somewhat regular edges, rap raw eggs sharply at their midpoint against the edge of a metal bowl. This makes for the cleanest break. The edges can be trimmed and further shaped with kitchen scissors if desired. One half of the shell of a hard-boiled egg can be used as well: Tap the small end of the egg on a hard surface to crack the shell, then peel it about two-thirds of the way down. Using a metal teaspoon, scoop out the cooked egg. With your fingers or scissors, shape the edge as desired.

Recycling Eggshells

Eggshells make excellent compost, so add them to your compost pile if you have one. If not, break the shells up, then dig them into the ground around your plants. They will eventually break down and add nutrients, especially calcium, to the soil.

whole eggs

2

Frisée Salad with Lardons and Poached Eggs

PALE, CREAM-COLORED LEAVES OF FRISÉE, TOSSED WITH CRISP BITS OF THICK BACON, THEN TOPPED
WITH A POACHED EGG AND SERVED WITH TOASTED SLICES OF OLIVE-OIL-DRIZZLED BAGUETTE, MAKE A CLASSIC LUNCH
OR SUPPERTIME DISH IN FRANCE, OR A FIRST COURSE FOR A LARGER MEAL. THE EGG, ONCE BROKEN,
BLENDS WITH THE VINAIGRETTE TO MAKE A CREAMY SAUCE FOR THE SALAD, PERFECT FOR BREAD DIPPING.

1/4 cup extra-virgin olive oil

2 tablespoons red wine vinegar

1/2 teaspoon salt

1/2 teaspoon freshly ground pepper

4 cups pale inner yellow leaves frisée from
about 2 heads

4 slices thick bacon, cut into 1/2-inch pieces

4 eggs

In a large salad bowl, mix the olive oil, vinegar, salt, and pepper together with a fork. Add the frisée, tossing to coat. Set aside.

In a medium skillet, fry the bacon over medium heat until crisp. Transfer to paper towels to drain. Add the bacon pieces to the salad, toss, and divide the dressed salad among 4 individual plates and set aside.

In a large saucepan, bring 2 inches of water to just under a boil, when tiny bubbles are forming around the edge. Reduce heat to medium. Break each egg carefully into a small dish and carefully lower the eggs into the water, separating them so they are not touching. Cover and cook for 4 or 5 minutes, or until the egg whites are opaque.

With a large slotted spoon, lift each egg out and put on top of each salad. Serve immediately. *Serves 4*

Oeufs Mimosa

OEUFS MIMOSA IS A CLASSIC FIRST COURSE IN FRENCH HOMES AND RESTAURANTS.
THESE HARD-BOILED EGGS ARE SERVED EITHER WHOLE, DRESSED WITH MAYONNAISE, AND TOPPED
WITH SIEVED EGG YOLKS AND MINCED EGG WHITES, OR THE EGGS ARE HALVED
AND STUFFED WITH THEIR EGG YOLKS, WHICH HAVE BEEN BLENDED AND FLUFFED WITH SPICY MUSTARD.
THIS IS AN IDEAL USE FOR EASTER EGGS ONCE THE HUNT IS OVER.

6 hard-boiled eggs

1 tablespoon Dijon mustard

1/2 teaspoon salt

1/2 teaspoon freshly ground pepper

2 tablespoons minced shallots

8 delicate lettuce leaves,
such as red leaf, green leaf, or butterhead

Cut the eggs in half lengthwise. Remove the yolks, put them in a medium bowl, and add the mustard, salt, pepper, and shallots. Using a fork, mash the yolk mixture until smooth and fluffy.

Spoon a heaping teaspoonful into the cavity of each egg half to make a mound.

Arrange the lettuce leaves on 4 individual plates and place 3 stuffed egg halves on each plate. *Serves 4*

Scotch Eggs

THESE EGGS ARE SERVED IN PUBS THROUGHOUT THE BRITISH ISLES. COATED WITH A LAYER
OF HERBED SAUSAGE, THEN DIPPED IN EGG AND BREAD CRUMBS, THE WHOLE HARD-BOILED EGGS ARE DEEP-FRIED
TO PRODUCE THE GOLDEN BROWN COATING THAT CHARACTERIZES THESE SAVORY TREATS.

4 ounces (1/2 cup) chicken or
pork bulk sausage

1 teaspoon minced fresh thyme

1 teaspoon minced fresh parsley

Vegetable oil for frying

6 hard-boiled eggs

1 egg, lightly beaten

2/3 cup fresh bread crumbs

In a medium bowl, combine the sausage, thyme, and parsley and mix well. Set aside.

Add 1 to 1-1/2 inches of oil to a wok, a deep, heavy pot, or a deep fryer. Heat over medium heat to 375°F.

Tightly press a 1/4-inch-thick layer of the sausage around each of the eggs; set aside. Dip each coated egg in the beaten egg, then roll in the bread crumbs to coat.

Using a slotted spoon, lower each egg into the hot oil and fry until golden brown, 1-1/2 to 2 minutes. Turn and cook on the second side until golden brown, about 2 minutes.

Using a slotted spoon, transfer the eggs to paper towels to drain. Serve hot or at room temperature. *Serves 6*

Huevos Rancheros

BREAKFAST MEXICAN STYLE OFTEN STARTS WITH A WARM TORTILLA SPREAD WITH REFRIED BEANS,

TOPPED WITH A FRIED EGG, AND LIBERALLY DRIZZLED WITH SPICY RED SAUCE. THIS ALSO MAKES A FESTIVE

SUPPER DISH. YOU CAN PURCHASE SALSA ALREADY PREPARED, ALTHOUGH THIS TASTY HOMEMADE

SALSA CAN BE MADE QUICKLY BEFORE STARTING TO COOK THE BEANS AND EGGS.

RANCHERO SALSA

2 tablespoons vegetable oil

2 tablespoons finely chopped onion

1 garlic clove, minced

1 tablespoon ground pasilla chili powder

1/2 cup (4 ounces) tomato paste

1/3 to 1/2 cup chicken broth

1-1/2 teaspoons minced fresh oregano or
1/2 teaspoon dried

1/4 teaspoon salt

30 ounces canned refried beans,
spicy or regular

1/4 cup water

12 corn tortillas

Vegetable oil for frying

4 or 8 eggs

To make the salsa: In a small skillet over medium-high heat, heat the oil and sauté the onions and garlic just until translucent. Stir in the ground chili, then add the remaining salsa ingredients. Reduce the heat to low and cook, stirring, for 7 to 8 minutes, or just long enough to blend the flavors. Remove from heat. Set aside and keep warm.

In a medium saucepan, heat the beans and water over medium-high heat, stirring often, until hot, about 6 or 7 minutes. Set aside and keep warm.

Heat a large, heavy skillet or griddle over high heat and add the tortillas one at a time, heating each a minute or two on each side to soften. Wrap in a towel to keep warm.

In the bottom of a large skillet over medium-low heat, heat a thin film of oil. Break the eggs into the pan (in batches if necessary) and then fry the eggs until the whites are firm and the yolks almost firm. Stack 1 or 2 tortillas on each of four plates. Spread with 2 or 3 heaping tablespoons of beans, then top with a fried egg. Drizzle with a tablespoon or so of salsa and serve immediately, accompanied by the remaining salsa and tortillas. *Serves 4*

Eggs Benedict with Roasted Balsamic Asparagus

EGGS BENEDICT IS AN AMERICAN CLASSIC, ELEGANT, AND SPECIAL. IT MAKES A PERFECT MOTHER'S DAY BREAKFAST
TO DELIVER BEDSIDE ON A BEAUTIFUL TRAY ALONG WITH FLOWERS, JUICE, AND COFFEE.

12 asparagus spears

1/4 cup balsamic vinegar

1 tablespoon extra-virgin olive oil

1/4 teaspoon salt

1/4 teaspoon freshly ground pepper

HOLLANDAISE SAUCE

1/2 cup (1 stick) unsalted butter

1-1/2 tablespoons fresh lemon juice

3 egg yolks

4 tablespoons boiling water

1/4 teaspoon salt

1/4 teaspoon cayenne pepper

4 English muffins, halved

4 thin slices Virginia or other ham

4 poached eggs (page 12)

Preheat the oven to 450°F. Place the asparagus spears in a shallow baking dish, pour the balsamic vinegar and olive oil over them, and sprinkle with salt and pepper. Turn the asparagus several times to coat the spears, then roast them, uncovered, for 15 to 20 minutes, turning several times until the asparagus is tender-crisp and the color has darkened slightly. Remove and cover loosely with aluminum foil. Set aside.

To make the sauce: In a medium saucepan, melt the butter over medium heat. In a small saucepan, warm the lemon juice over low heat. In a double boiler, heat the egg yolks over barely simmering water that does not touch the bottom of the upper pan. Whisk the yolks constantly until they begin to thicken, then add 1 tablespoon of the boiling water. Continue to whisk until the yolks have thickened, which takes only seconds. Repeat, adding the remaining boiling water 1 tablespoon at a time. Whisk in the warm lemon juice and remove the pan from heat. Pour in the melted butter very slowly, whisking constantly, and add the salt and the cayenne. The sauce will become thick.

To serve, toast the English muffins. Place a muffin half on each of 4 plates and top each with a slice of ham, 3 asparagus spears, and 1 poached egg. Spoon 1/4 cup sauce over each egg. Place one of the remaining muffin halves on each plate and serve immediately. *Serves 4*

Quail Eggs with Caviar

MINCED, HARD-BOILED EGG YOLKS AND WHITES ARE CLASSIC TOPPINGS FOR
RUSSIAN CAVIAR, ALONG WITH SOUR CREAM AND MINCED ONION. HERE, THE ORDER
IS REVERSED: TINY, HARD-BOILED QUAIL EGGS ARE LIGHTLY SPREAD WITH
SOUR CREAM AND SPRINKLED WITH ONIONS BEFORE BEING TOPPED WITH CAVIAR.

12 quail eggs, hard-boiled for 5 minutes then chilled

1/4 cup chilled sour cream

1/2 yellow onion, minced and chilled

1/2 ounce chilled caviar

Cut the eggs in half crosswise. Spread the cut end of each half
with about 1/4 teaspoon sour cream, then add 1/8 teaspoon
minced onion and top with about 1/4 teaspoon caviar. Serve
immediately. *Serves 4*

Eggs in Tarragon and White-Wine Aspic

WHOLE HARD-BOILED EGGS, SET IN A GLISTENING COAT OF ASPIC, ARE A SPECIALTY FOUND AT FRENCH *TRAITEURS*,
OR DELICATESSENS, BUT THEY ARE EASILY MADE IN THE HOME KITCHEN FOR A GLAMOROUS AND FLAVORFUL FIRST COURSE.
CLARIFYING THE BROTH WITH EGG WHITES IS NECESSARY TO ACHIEVE A CLEAR, UNCLOUDED ASPIC.

ASPIC

3 cups chicken broth

1-1/2 cups dry white wine

1/4 cup fresh tarragon sprigs, plus 24 leaves

2 carrots, peeled and finely chopped

2 leeks, whites only, finely chopped

2 celery stalks, finely chopped

3 egg whites, beaten until just frothy

2-1/2 tablespoons (2-1/2 envelopes) plain gelatin

8 hard-boiled eggs

8 large butterhead lettuce leaves

Homemade or purchased mayonnaise for garnish

8 fresh tarragon sprigs for garnish

In a large saucepan, combine the broth and wine and bring to a boil over medium-high heat. Meanwhile, in a large bowl, combine the 1/4 cup tarragon, carrots, leeks, celery, and egg whites and mix well.

Pour the hot broth into the bowl with the vegetables and egg whites and stir together. Pour the contents of the bowl back into the saucepan, bring to a boil over medium heat, and cook, whisking often, for about 5 minutes or until frothy. As the mixture boils, a soft mass will form on the top. If necessary to release steam, use a spoon to make a vent hole in the mass. Reduce heat to low and simmer, uncovered, for 30 to 40 minutes.

Line a sieve with a damp dish towel or several layers of cheesecloth and place it over a medium bowl, preferably spouted. Using a spoon, break up the crust that has formed on the broth, then pour the broth through the sieve into the bowl.

In a small bowl, combine the gelatin and 3 tablespoons of the hot broth. Pour the gelatin mixture into the bowl of broth and stir well, until the gelatin is dissolved. Pour a 1/4-inch-thick layer of the mixture into eight 1-1/2-cup soufflé dishes. Refrigerate the dishes until the gelatin layer is firm, about 15 minutes. Place a hard-boiled egg in each mold and pour about 1/2 cup of the gelatin mixture over it. Top with 3 tarragon leaves. Return to the refrigerator to chill until firm, at least 3 or 4 hours.

To serve, place a lettuce leaf on each of 8 salad plates. To unmold the aspic, place the molds in a shallow pan and pour boiling water in the pan around them. Let stand for 20 seconds, then remove from the water. Invert a salad plate over a mold, and holding the plate and mold tightly together, invert the mold. The aspic will turn out onto the plate. Repeat with the remaining molds. Garnish each plate with a spoonful of mayonnaise and a sprig of tarragon. *Serves 8*

Eggs Pickled with Tea and Star Anise

TEA, THE NATIONAL DRINK OF CHINA, IS COMBINED HERE WITH STAR ANISE, A POPULAR CHINESE SPICE, AND RICE-WINE VINEGAR TO PRODUCE DELICATELY FLAVORED EGGS TO SERVE AS A GARNISH OR AS PART OF AN APPETIZER PLATE. AS THE EGGS MARINATE, THEY BECOME A PALE CREAM COLOR WITH DARKER MARBLING AND VEINING WHERE THE SHELL WAS CRACKED.

1 cup plain rice-wine vinegar

1-1/2 cups water

2 tablespoons black tea leaves

3 star anise pods

1 tablespoon honey

6 unshelled hard-boiled eggs

In a medium saucepan, bring the vinegar and water to a boil over medium-high heat. Add the tea, star anise, and honey and stir. Put the eggs in a medium bowl and pour the hot mixture over them to cover completely. Let cool. Cover and refrigerate for 2 to 4 days before serving. *Serves 6*

Lemon-Butter Easter Egg Cookies with Royal Icing

COOKIES CUT OUT IN EGG SHAPES AND BRIGHTLY DECORATED WITH ICING MAKE SPECIAL EASTER HOLIDAY TREATS.

1-3/4 cups sifted all-purpose flour

1/2 teaspoon baking powder

1/4 teaspoon salt

2/3 cups (1-1/3 sticks) unsalted
butter at room temperature

1/2 cup granulated sugar

1 egg

1 teaspoon fresh lemon juice

2 tablespoons grated lemon zest

ROYAL ICING

2 egg whites

1 pound (4 cups) confectioners' sugar,
plus more as needed

1 teaspoon water (optional)

Food coloring as desired

Preheat the oven to 400°F. Sift the flour, baking powder, and salt together onto a piece of waxed paper. In a medium bowl, cream the butter and sugar together until light and fluffy. Beat in the egg, lemon juice, and lemon zest. Add the flour mixture in thirds, stirring each time until the dough is smooth.

On a lightly floured board, roll the dough out to a thickness of 1/8 inch. Cut into the desired cookie shapes and put them on ungreased baking sheets. Gather up the scraps of dough and roll them out to use all the dough. To hang the cookies on a cookie tree later, make a 1/4-inch-diameter hole in each cookie using an ice pick.

Bake until just lightly browned on the bottom and pale golden on top, 6 to 8 minutes. Remove from the oven and let the cookies cool on the sheets for 5 minutes, then transfer them to wire racks.

To make the icing: In a large bowl, using an electric mixer, beat the egg whites and sugar together for about 10 minutes, or until stiff enough to spread. If the icing is too stiff, add 1 teaspoon of water and beat. If it is too thin, continue beating another 2 or 3 minutes, or add another 1/4 cup of confectioners' sugar and beat.

To make different colored icings, divide the icing among several bowls and add food coloring as desired. Using a knife or spatula, spread the icing on the cookies. *Makes about 36 cookies*

tabletop eggs

3

Egg Napkin Rings

EGGS WITH PARTYGOERS' NAMES CREATE A PERSONAL,

YET FUN AND INFORMAL LOOK FOR A PARTY TABLE.

YOU WILL NEED:

Dyed, hollowed eggs

Sharp pencil

Black ultra-fine-point permanent marker

Pearl-headed hat pins

Hot-glue gun and glue sticks

12-inch lengths of 1-inch-wide ribbon, such as satin, grosgrain, silk, or organdy

TO MAKE:

Using the pencil, write each name in a curly script on the center of each egg. Erase any errors.

Using the permanent marker, retrace the names, adding thicker strokes where desired. To prevent smearing, avoid touching the areas of lettering while finishing the script.

At one end of a length of ribbon, tie a small bow and stick a hat pin through it.

Place a pea-sized dot of hot glue over the hole in the pointed end of the egg.

Insert the hat pin into the hole. Press the bow gently into the glue until it dries and the bow is securely glued to the egg.

Wrap the remaining ribbon tail around a napkin. Place an egg napkin holder at each setting on your holiday table so that each guest can take one home as a memento of the event.

Flowering Easter Basket Centerpiece

THIS COLORFUL SPRINGTIME BASKET CAN BE QUICKLY PREPARED TO GRACE YOUR TABLE FOR AN EASTER BRUNCH.

YOU WILL NEED:

Wire basket

Sheet moss (available at craft stores)

1 medium-size, plastic kitchen trash bag

Scissors

Branches or thick vines

Florist wire (available at craft stores)

2 flats of 3-inch pots of pansies
(available at garden centers)

1 dozen dyed eggs

TO MAKE:

Line the basket with moss on the bottom and sides.

Line the moss with 2 layers of the kitchen bag, and with the scissors, trim the edge of the bag so it doesn't show above the moss.

Twist the branches or vines around each other to make a handle for the basket and cut them to length. Wrap the ends of the handle with florist wire and secure them to the sides of the basket.

Fill the basket with the pansies and place eggs among the flowers.

Eggshell Vases

THESE DELICATE VASES FILLED WITH PETITE FLOWERS CAN

BE USED TO STYLE INDIVIDUAL TABLE SETTINGS.

YOU WILL NEED:

Hollowed turkey eggs
(available from florist supply stores)

Strong pin or needle

Bowl-shaped dessert dishes

Hot-glue gun and glue sticks

Flowers with small blooms
such as lilies-of-the-valley, muscari, lilac sprigs,
and dwarf narcissus

TO MAKE:

Use the pin or needle to enlarge the hole in the narrow end of each eggshell until a finger can be inserted, then crack off and remove the top third of the shell.

Fill each eggshell two-thirds full with water and place in a dessert dish filled with water.

If an eggshell does not stay upright, empty the dessert dish, dry it, hot-glue the eggshell to the dish, and refill it.

Arrange the flowers in the shells.

Egg and Nest Centerpiece

A COLLECTION OF UNDECORATED EGGS IN A NATURAL
DISPLAY SETS A RUSTIC FARMHOUSE TONE FOR THE TABLE.

YOU WILL NEED:

Assorted eggs (quail, pheasant, duck, and chicken)
in different colors (available at craft stores,
farmers' markets, and specialty food stores)

Bird's nests (found outdoors or available
at craft stores and florist supply stores)

Bowls, pedestal dishes, egg cups

TO MAKE:

Fill the nests with eggs and put some nests in pedestal dishes
and others nearby on the table. Place eggs in bowls and egg
cups, then cluster them around the nests.

egg scrambles & sauces

4

Artichoke Frittata

FRITTATAS ARE THICK ITALIAN OMELETTES, FREQUENTLY MADE WITH SEASONAL VEGETABLES,

SUCH AS ARTICHOKES OR ASPARAGUS IN SPRING AND WILD MUSHROOMS OR SWEET RED PEPPERS IN FALL.

THEY ARE EASY TO MAKE AND OFFER AN IMPRESSIVE PRESENTATION.

6 eggs

2 tablespoons half-and-half

1/4 cup grated Parmesan cheese

3/4 teaspoon salt

1/2 teaspoon freshly ground pepper

1 tablespoon butter

1 tablespoon extra-virgin olive oil

1/4 yellow onion, finely chopped

1 garlic clove, minced

2 cups water-packed or
frozen artichoke hearts, drained and
cut lengthwise into quarters

1/4 cup chopped fresh
flat-leaf parsley

1 tablespoon chopped fresh
thyme leaves

In a large bowl, beat the eggs, half-and-half, cheese, salt, and pepper together until just blended. In a 10-inch skillet, melt the butter with the olive oil over medium-high heat. When the butter foams, add the onion and sauté for 3 to 4 minutes. Add the garlic and sauté for 1 minute.

Distribute the artichoke hearts evenly over the bottom of the skillet, then pour the egg mixture over them. Reduce heat to low and cook until the eggs are just firm around the edges, about 3 or 4 minutes. Using a spatula, lift the edges of the eggs and tilt the skillet to let the uncooked eggs run beneath. Continue cooking another 4 to 5 minutes, or until the egg mixture on top is nearly set. As an alternative, cook the top under a broiler.

Invert a plate on top of the skillet, and holding the platter and the skillet together firmly with pot holders, flip them, turning the frittata out onto the plate. Sprinkle half the herbs into the skillet, then slide the frittata back into the skillet with the cooked side up. Cook another 1 to 2 minutes. Invert a flat serving plate over the pan, and flip them as above. Sprinkle with the remaining herbs. Cut into wedges and serve immediately or at room temperature. *Serves 4*

Egg Curds with Sautéed Mushrooms

TENDER MUSHROOMS AND BITS OF TARRAGON FLAVOR A DISH OF SMALL-CURD SCRAMBLED EGGS

THAT CAN OFTEN BE FOUND ON ELEGANTLY SET ENGLISH BRUNCH TABLES.

3 tablespoons butter

3 ounces mushrooms, thinly sliced

8 eggs

1 teaspoon salt

1/2 teaspoon freshly ground pepper

2 tablespoons crème fraîche or
sour cream

1 tablespoon minced fresh tarragon

In a medium skillet, melt 1 tablespoon of the butter over medium heat. When the butter foams, add the mushrooms and sauté for 2 to 3 minutes, or until just lightly golden. Set aside.

In a large bowl, beat the eggs with the salt and pepper until just blended. In a large skillet, melt the remaining 2 tablespoons of butter over medium heat. When the butter foams, pour in the egg mixture. Reduce heat to low and stir constantly until almost cooked to the desired consistency, about 5 to 6 minutes for a soft curd, 7 to 8 for a firmer one. Drain the mushrooms and stir them in along with the crème fraîche and half the tarragon. Cook for 1 minute, stirring constantly. Serve immediately on warm plates, garnished with the remaining tarragon. *Serves 3 to 4*

Egg Foo Yong

THIS IS NOT A DISH FROM CHINA, BUT A CULTURAL HYBRID FOUND ON THE MENU
OF EVERY CHINESE-AMERICAN RESTAURANT IN THE 1950S AND 1960S. THE EGGS ARE MIXED WITH BEAN SPROUTS
AND SHRIMP OR BITS OF COOKED PORK, THEN FRIED IN PATTIES AND SERVED WITH A THICKENED SOY SAUCE.
THIS MAKES A DELICIOUS LUNCH OR SUPPER DISH, OR A SIDE DISH.

7 eggs, lightly beaten

2 cups fresh bean sprouts

8 ounces bay shrimp, peeled, deveined, cooked, and
chopped

1/2 teaspoon salt

1/2 teaspoon freshly ground pepper

Vegetable oil for frying

SAUCE

2 tablespoons cornstarch

1/2 cup water

2 tablespoons low-salt soy sauce

3/4 cup finely chopped green onions for garnish

In a large bowl, combine the eggs, bean sprouts, shrimp, salt, and pepper and beat until well blended.

Coat a large skillet with a thin film of vegetable oil and heat over medium heat. Drop 1/2 cupfuls of the egg mixture into the pan to make patties, leaving about 2 inches between them. Cook for 3 or 4 minutes, or until lightly golden and firm on the bottom. With a spatula, turn them and cook until golden and firm on the other side, about 2 or 3 minutes. Transfer to a platter and keep warm. Repeat until all the egg mixture is used.

While the patties are cooking, make the sauce: In a small bowl, stir the cornstarch into the water. In a small saucepan, bring the soy sauce to a boil over medium-high heat. Stir in the cornstarch mixture and cook until thickened, about 1 or 2 minutes. Set aside and keep warm.

To serve, arrange the patties on the platter or on individual serving plates. Spoon the sauce over them, top with a sprinkling of green onions, and serve immediately. *Serves 4*

Brouillade with Truffles

THIS IS THE PREMIERE SCRAMBLED-EGG DISH, A FRENCH CONCOCTION PERFUMED WITH BITS OF EARTHY, AROMATIC BLACK TRUFFLES, ONE OF THE GREATEST OF DELICACIES. IT IS WORTH MAKING A SPECIAL EFFORT TO FIND FARM-FRESH EGGS FOR THIS DISH AT A FARMERS' MARKET OR A COUNTRY PRODUCE STAND. THEIR FLAVOR AND BRILLIANT GOLDEN COLOR ENHANCE THE EXTRAORDINARY AROMA OF THE TRUFFLES, WHICH ARE AT THEIR PEAK OF FLAVOR IN LATE JANUARY AND FEBRUARY.

8 eggs

1 ounce fresh black truffles, scrubbed and minced

1/2 cup (1 stick) of unsalted butter,
cut into 1-inch pieces

1 teaspoon salt

2 teaspoons freshly ground white pepper

Crack the eggs into a bowl and add the truffles. In the top part of a double boiler, whisk the eggs and truffles together. Add the butter and place over simmering water. Whisk constantly until the mixture has thickened into a creamy mass of tiny curds; this will take about 15 minutes. Whisk in the salt and pepper and serve immediately on warmed plates, accompanied by slices of baguette or other country-style bread, plain or toasted. *Serves 3 or 4 as a first course, 2 as a main course*

Pad Thai

ONE OF THE GREAT NOODLE DISHES OF THAILAND, PAD THAI CAN BE MADE WITH SHRIMP, PORK, BEEF, OR FRESH BEAN CURD.

8 ounces rice stick noodles, 1/4 inch wide

SAUCE

1/4 cup fresh lemon juice

2 serrano chilies, minced

1 tablespoon Thai fish sauce

SEASONING MIXTURE

2 tablespoons plain rice-wine vinegar

2 tablespoons Thai fish sauce

3 tablespoons granulated sugar

1 teaspoon tomato paste

2 ounces preserved fermented bean curd

3 tablespoons vegetable oil

2 garlic cloves, minced

8 dried shrimp, crumbled

1/4 cup dried salted radish, finely chopped

8 ounces medium shrimp (about 20), peeled and deveined

2 eggs

2-1/2 cups fresh bean sprouts

1/2 cup coarsely chopped fresh cilantro

1/2 cup unsalted, roasted peanuts

6 green onions, including half the greens, quartered lengthwise and cut into 1-inch lengths

2 limes, quartered

Place noodles in a large bowl and add warm water to cover.

In a small bowl, combine all the sauce ingredients. Mix well and set aside.

In a small bowl, combine all the seasoning mixture ingredients and stir until blended. Set aside. Cut the bean curd into thin strips about 1/4-inch wide and 1-inch long. Set aside.

In a wok or large, heavy skillet over medium-high heat, heat the vegetable oil. When it is very hot, add the garlic and stir-fry for about 20 seconds. Add the bean curd, dried shrimp, and dried radish and stir-fry for 1 to 2 minutes. Add the whole shrimp and cook until just pink, about 1 minute. Stir in the seasoning mixture. Push the shrimp to the side of the pan and break in one of the eggs, stirring for about 30 seconds, then push it to the side with the shrimp. Add the noodles and toss everything together. Make a well in the center and break in the second egg. Let it cook without stirring until it begins to firm, about 30 seconds, then toss again. Add 1-1/2 cups of the bean sprouts, half the cilantro, and half the peanuts. Toss and cook for 30 seconds. Transfer to a platter.

Serve hot, garnished with the remaining bean sprouts, cilantro, and peanuts and the green onions, accompanied by the limes and the sauce. *Serves 4*

Sautéed Peppers and Onions Wrapped in Spanish Tortillas

A SPANISH-STYLE TORTILLA IS A THIN, FLAT OMELETTE, NOT THE FAMILIAR MEXICAN TORTILLA MADE FROM CORN OR FLOUR. THEY ARE A STAPLE IN SPAIN, WHERE THEY ARE MADE WITH ALL KINDS OF DIFFERENT VEGETABLES, OFTEN WITH BITS OF SHRIMP, MUSSELS, OR CRUMBLED SAUSAGE ADDED HERE.

FILLING

2 tablespoons extra-virgin olive oil

2 garlic cloves, minced

2 yellow onions, cut into 1/4-inch-thick slices

4 large red bell peppers, seeded, deribbed, and cut into 1/4-inch-wide strips

1/4 teaspoon salt

1/4 teaspoon freshly ground pepper

1 tablespoon minced fresh oregano or marjoram leaves

1 teaspoon minced fresh thyme leaves

SPANISH TORTILLAS

6 eggs

1/2 teaspoon salt

1/2 teaspoon freshly ground pepper

1 tablespoon butter

1 tablespoon extra-virgin olive oil

To make the filling: In a large skillet over medium-high heat, heat the olive oil. Add the garlic and sauté for 1 to 2 minutes. Add the onions and peppers and sauté for 4 to 5 minutes, or until the vegetables are limp. Stir in the salt and pepper. Reduce heat to low, cover, and cook for 15 minutes. Set aside. Just before serving, stir in the oregano and thyme.

To make the tortillas: Preheat the broiler. In a medium bowl, beat the eggs, salt, and pepper together just until blended. In a 12-inch ovenproof skillet, melt the butter with the olive oil over medium heat. When the butter foams, pour in half the egg mixture, reduce heat to low, and cook for 2 to 3 minutes, or until the eggs have set slightly. Lift the edges with a spatula and tilt the pan to allow some of the uncooked egg to slide underneath. Cook for 1 to 1-1/2 minutes, then slip under a broiler for 1 to 2 minutes until the top of the eggs are set and the edges firm and pulled away slightly from the skillet. Slip a spatula all around and underneath to loosen the tortilla. Tilt the skillet and slide the tortilla onto a warm plate. Keep warm in a low oven while repeating to cook the second tortilla.

To serve, spoon several tablespoons filling over half of a tortilla and gently fold it over on itself. Do the same with the second tortilla. Serve hot, warm, or at room temperature. *Serves 4 as a first course, 2 as a main course; makes two 12-inch tortillas.*

Folded Omelette with Basil and Tomato

THIS IS A WONDERFUL OMELETTE TO MAKE IN SUMMER, USING VINE-RIPENED TOMATOES AND FRESH BASIL. IF POSSIBLE, USE TOMATOES OF DIFFERENT COLORS, AND PURPLE BASIL FOR FURTHER COLOR CONTRAST.

1 pound tomatoes, preferably a mix of red and yellow, peeled, seeded, and diced

3/4 teaspoon salt

1 teaspoon freshly ground pepper

1/4 cup chopped fresh purple or green basil, plus several sprigs for garnish

6 eggs

1-1/2 tablespoons butter

In a medium bowl, combine the tomatoes with 1/4 teaspoon of the salt, 1/2 teaspoon of the pepper, and the chopped basil. Set aside.

In a medium bowl, beat the eggs with the remaining 1/2 teaspoon salt and 1/2 teaspoon pepper until just blended. In a 12-inch skillet, melt the butter over medium heat. When it foams, add the eggs and stir until they begin to thicken, just a few seconds. Reduce heat to low. As the eggs set along the side, lift the edges with a spatula and tip the pan to let the uncooked egg run beneath. Continue to cook until the omelette is set, 30 to 40 seconds longer, depending on whether a slightly runny or a firm omelette is preferred. The bottom should be slightly golden.

Spread the tomato mixture on one half of the omelette leaving a 1-inch border on the edge. Slip a spatula under the uncoated half, and pulling the pan up and toward you, flip the uncoated half over the covered half. Cook another 30 to 40 seconds. Transfer to a warm plate. Cut into pieces and serve immediately, garnished with basil sprigs. *Serves 3 to 4*

Folded Dessert Omelette with Orange Marmalade

IN A PUFFY OR SOUFFLÉ OMELETTE, THE EGG WHITES AND YOLKS ARE BEATEN SEPARATELY, THEN THE WHITES
ARE FOLDED INTO THE YOLKS AND THE AIRY MIXTURE IS IMMEDIATELY COOKED. THE OMELETTE PUFFS TO LOFTY HEIGHTS,
THEN IS FINISHED IN THE OVEN AND FOLDED IN HALF TO ENCASE A FILLING.

3 eggs, separated

6 tablespoons granulated sugar

1/4 teaspoon salt

1 tablespoon butter

2 tablespoons orange marmalade, warmed

Preheat the oven to 350°F. In a medium bowl, beat or whisk the egg yolks with the sugar and salt until pale in color. In a large bowl, beat the egg whites until soft peaks form. Fold the egg whites into the egg yolks until just blended.

In a 9- or 10-inch ovenproof skillet, melt the butter over medium heat. When the butter foams, pour the egg mixture into the skillet and spread it evenly. Reduce heat to low and cook for 2 to 3 minutes, or until the bottom of the omelette is slightly browned and the edges have begun to puff.

Place the pan in the oven and cook until the omelette is puffed and faintly golden, 5 to 6 minutes. Remove from the oven and drizzle the warm marmalade down the center. Slip a spatula first under one edge and then beneath the omelette and fold one half on top of the other. The outer edges may not meet. Slide the folded omelette onto a warm plate and serve immediately. *Serves 1 to 2*

Pain Perdu

THE FRENCH ARE CREDITED WITH HAVING ORIGINATED *PAIN PERDU*,
OR FRENCH TOAST, BY DREDGING SLICES OF DAY-OLD BREAD IN EGG AND THEN
FRYING THEM IN BUTTER. ANY MANNER OF BREAD, SUCH AS CROISSANTS,
RAISIN BREAD, OR SLICES OF BRIOCHE CAN BE USED.

4 eggs

1 tablespoon granulated sugar

3/4 teaspoon salt

1/2 teaspoon grated nutmeg

3 day-old croissants, halved horizontally

2 tablespoons unsalted butter

1 cup blackberry or strawberry preserves

In a shallow bowl, beat the eggs, sugar, salt, and nutmeg together until just blended. Soak the croissant slices in the egg mixture on both sides. In a large skillet, melt the butter over medium heat. Place the croissant halves in the skillet and fry for 3 to 4 minutes, or until browned. Turn and fry on the second side. Serve hot, accompanied by the preserves.
Serves 4 to 6

Creamed Eggs, Ham, and Mushrooms on Toast

THIS IS A CLASSIC DISH TO MAKE THE DAY AFTER EASTER WITH DECORATED, HARD-BOILED EGGS
THAT HAVE BEEN COLLECTED AND REFRIGERATED.

BÉCHAMEL SAUCE

2 tablespoons unsalted butter

2 tablespoons all-purpose flour

1/4 teaspoon ground nutmeg

1 teaspoon freshly ground pepper

1/8 teaspoon cayenne pepper

3/4 teaspoon salt

3/4 cup milk

1 tablespoon butter

8 ounces mushrooms,
cut into thick slices

1/4 teaspoon salt

1 pound ham, cut into 1/2-inch dice

2 tablespoons minced fresh parsley

5 hard-boiled eggs,
cut crosswise into thick slices

6 slices toast

1 teaspoon paprika

To make the sauce: In a medium, heavy saucepan, melt the butter over medium heat. When the butter foams, remove the pan from heat and whisk in the flour, nutmeg, pepper, cayenne pepper, and salt until a thick paste forms. Return the pan to medium heat and gradually whisk in the milk in a steady stream. Cook for 2 to 3 minutes, stirring constantly. Reduce heat to low and simmer, stirring occasionally, until the sauce thickens, about 10 to 15 minutes.

In a small skillet, melt the butter over medium heat. When it foams, add the mushrooms and sprinkle with the salt. Sauté for 2 to 3 minutes, or until lightly golden. Drain the mushrooms and stir them into the sauce along with the ham and parsley. Reserving 4 attractive slices for a garnish, gently stir in the eggs. Cook for about 2 minutes, or just enough to thoroughly heat the ham and the eggs.

Place 1 slice of toast on each of 4 plates. Divide the creamed eggs evenly among the 4 plates, spooning them over the toast. Cut the remaining 2 slices of toast diagonally into 4 triangles each. Place 2 triangles on each plate and garnish with the remaining sliced eggs and the paprika. Serve at once. *Serves 4*

Asparagus and Potatoes with Avgolemono Sauce

THIS GREEK LEMON AND EGG SAUCE, FROTHY AND LIGHT AS AIR, IS SERVED THROUGHOUT THAT COUNTRY
WITH A MULTITUDE OF DISHES, INCLUDING FISH, MEATS, AND SOUPS.

2 pounds asparagus

2-1/2 pounds red or white rose
potatoes (about 8 potatoes)

3 eggs, separated

1/2 teaspoon salt

3 tablespoons fresh lemon juice

1-1/2 cups chicken broth

1 tablespoon cornstarch mixed
with 2 teaspoons water

Steam the asparagus in a covered pot over boiling water until just tender, 4 to 5 minutes. Rinse under cold water. Set aside.

Cook the potatoes in salted, boiling water for 20 to 25 minutes, or until tender when pierced with a fork. Drain and let cool to the touch. Using a knife, remove the potato skins and discard. Keep the potatoes warm while making the sauce.

In a large bowl, beat the egg whites and salt until soft peaks form. In a medium bowl, beat the egg yolks and lemon juice until just blended. Stir the egg yolks into the egg whites and set aside.

In a medium saucepan, heat the chicken broth over medium heat. Stir in the cornstarch mixture and cook for 2 minutes, stirring. Remove from heat and let cool to lukewarm. Gradually pour the broth into the eggs, whisking constantly. Pour the mixture into the saucepan. Cook over medium-low heat, whisking constantly, until thickened, 3 to 4 minutes. Do not boil or the sauce will curdle.

Arrange the asparagus and the potatoes on a platter and pour half the sauce over them.

Serve the remaining sauce alongside. *Serves 6*

eggs for kids

5

Crepe Paper Flower Baskets

DECORATING THESE SIMPLE BASKETS IS NOT DIFFICULT FOR LITTLE FINGERS, AND THE RESULTS ARE INDIVIDUALISTIC AND HIGHLY REWARDING.

YOU WILL NEED:

Crepe paper in dark green and other bright colors

Scissors

Florist covered wire cut into 24-inch lengths

Hot-glue gun and glue

Basket

TO MAKE:

STEP 1 For the foliage, cut one 2-by-12-inch strip of dark-green crepe paper. Down one side, cut slits 1-1/2-inches deep, and about 1/8-inch apart.

For the petals, cut five 1-by-6-inch strips of brightly colored crepe paper. For the flower center, cut one 1-by-6-inch strip of different-colored crepe paper.

Pinch the middle of each petal strip and twist the ends once. Fold the strip at the middle to make the ends meet, then twist the ends. Repeat with the flower center.

STEP 2 Put the twisted strips together to form a flower, with the flower center strip in the middle of the petal strips.

Use the middle of the wire to wrap the petal strips and the flower center strip together at their base, leaving two 6-inch ends of the wire for the stem.

Wrap the ends of the stem wire with the green paper foliage strip, hot-gluing it at the base of the flower to secure the paper.

Repeat to make more flowers.

STEP 3 Twist the stems of individual flowers together to make a garland.

STEP 4 Wire the garland around the rim of the basket, or wire individual flowers to the basket.

Paper Lattice-Covered Baskets

GEOMETRIC DESIGNS ARE REVEALED BY THE WEAVE OF THE MULTICOLORED PAPERS

USED ON THESE EGG-GATHERING BASKETS.

YOU WILL NEED:

Sheets of colored wrapping paper

10-inch round hard cardboard box

Paper glue

Paper-hole punch or ice pick

2 12-inch pieces of 1/2-inch wide trim or rickrack

Easter grass or wheatberry grass
(available in craft stores or florist supply stores)

TO MAKE:

Cut the paper into 1-by-24-inch strips.

Place the box upside down on a work surface.

Hold one strip of paper diagonally along the side of the box and glue 1 inch of the end to the bottom of the box.

Hold a second strip of the same paper parallel to the first strip with a 3/4-inch gap between them and glue its end likewise to the bottom of the box. Continue with other strips of the same paper until the box has been encircled.

Using a strip of a different color, hold it at a diagonal opposite to the diagonal of the first strips and glue 1 inch of its end to the bottom of the box. Repeat, continuing until the box is encircled.

Weave the strips, one over the other, working your way around the box and eventually turning it over.

Cut the excess paper from the strip, leaving 1-inch ends. Fold the ends over the top rim of the box and glue them to the inside of the rim.

With the paper-hole punch, make 2 holes on each side of the rim of the box, 1 inch below the rim and 2 inches apart. String the ends of the trim through the holes and knot the ends to make the handles.

Cut a 3-inch wide strip of paper and glue it to the inside of the box at the top to form an edging or a collar.

Fill with Easter grass or wheatberry grass.

Paper Cone Easter Baskets

YOU WILL NEED:

12-by-24-inch sheets of heavy construction paper

Scissors

Hot-glue gun and glue sticks

Fabric trimming (ribbon or seam binding)

Stapler and staples

Assorted buttons

Easter grass

TO MAKE:

Roll a sheet of paper into a cone, fold the top in to make an even rim, and secure the shape with hot glue down the seam.

Cut a length of fabric trimming and hot-glue it around the rim. Cut another length to use as a handle and glue its ends to the rim. Staple handle to cone for extra durability. Glue on decorative buttons to cover staples. Fill with Easter grass.

Mexican Cascarones

CASCARONES ARE DYED EGGS MEANT TO BE BROKEN OVER THE HEAD OF A FRIEND, SPILLING CONFETTI AND FAVORS.

CHILDREN TAKE SPECIAL DELIGHT NOT ONLY IN DECORATING THE EGGS BUT ALSO IN SMASHING THEM LATER.

YOU WILL NEED:

Egg dyes, hot water, distilled
white vinegar

Raw eggs

Small bowls or cups

Spoons

Empty egg carton

Scissors

Colored tissue paper

Egg cutter or sharp knife

Trinkets, candy, confetti, or rice

Clear paper glue

TO MAKE:

Prepare several colors of egg dye with hot water and vinegar in small bowls. Dye the eggs in assorted colors as desired. Lift eggs out with spoons and let dry in the egg carton.

While the eggs are drying, use scissors to cut out several 1- or 2-inch square pieces of tissue paper, one for each egg.

With the egg cutter or a sharp knife, cut off 1/6 of each egg from its narrow end and pour out the yolk and white. Rinse the inside of the shells and let them dry.

Fill each dried eggshell with trinkets, candy, confetti, or rice. Cover the hole of each egg with a piece of tissue paper and glue the edges to the shell.

If desired, cut narrow strips of tissue paper and glue them on the shell for decoration.

Sticker and Wax Crayon Decorated Eggs

USING COLORFUL STICKERS AND WAX CRAYONS IS THE SIMPLEST WAY

TO DECORATE EGGS AND IS IDEAL FOR VERY SMALL CHILDREN.

YOU WILL NEED:

Egg dyes, hot water, distilled white vinegar

Small bowls or cups

Hard-cooked eggs

Spoons

Empty egg carton

Stickers

Wax crayons

TO MAKE:

Prepare several colors of egg dye with hot water and vinegar in small bowls. Place some of the eggs in the dye until they are the desired hue, then remove them with spoons and let them dry in the egg carton. Apply the stickers.

Use the wax crayons on the undyed eggs to draw shapes or pictures on the shell, then dye the eggs in the various colors. The wax-covered areas will remain white when the eggs are removed from the dye.

Tie-Dyed Eggs

RUBBER BANDS AND TAPE CREATE
COMPLEX PATTERNS IN AN EGG-DYING
METHOD THAT IS NOT OVERLY COMPLEX
FOR CHILDREN TO DO.

YOU WILL NEED:

Egg dyes, hot water, distilled white
vinegar

Small bowls or cups

Hard-cooked white or brown eggs

Rubber bands, assorted narrow and wide

OR

1/4-inch-wide masking tape

Scissors

Spoons

Empty egg cartons

TO MAKE:

STEP 1 Prepare several colors of
egg dye with hot water and vinegar
in small bowls. Wrap undyed or
lightly dyed eggs with several rubber bands or pieces of tape, then
place them in the dye until they are
the desired color.

STEP 2 Remove the eggs from the
dye with spoons and let them dry in
the egg cartons, then remove the
rubber bands or tape.

Wrap the dyed eggs again with
rubber bands or tape in a different
pattern, or leave off entirely.

STEP 3 Put them in the same dye
or a different color.

STEP 4 Alternate the eggs in different dyes and different wraps, or no
wraps, in later dyes.

fillings, wraps & custards

6

Spring-Onion Egg Salad with Edible Blossoms

AN AMERICAN SODA-FOUNTAIN FAVORITE DURING THE 1940S AND 1950S, EGG SALAD SANDWICHES REMAIN

A LUNCH COUNTER STANDBY, ESPECIALLY WHEN SERVED WITH POTATO CHIPS AND SWEET PICKLES. MORE ELEGANT VERSIONS,

LIKE THIS FLOWER-STREWN ONE, ARE DESTINED FOR SPECIAL LUNCHES AND TEAS.

1/3 cup homemade or store-bought mayonnaise

1 teaspoon Dijon mustard

1/4 teaspoon salt

1/4 teaspoon freshly ground pepper

2 teaspoons sweet pickle juice

4 hard-boiled eggs, coarsely chopped

3 tablespoons minced green onion

4 slices homemade-style white or wheat bread

4 to 6 butterhead lettuce leaves

1/2 cup onion sprouts

1/4 mixed edible flower petals

In a medium bowl, stir the mayonnaise, mustard, salt, pepper, and pickle juice together, mixing well. Add the chopped eggs and green onion, folding them gently into the mayonnaise mixture.

Spread each slice of bread on one side with the mayonnaise mixture, then place a lettuce leaf on each to cover it fully, using bits of the extra leaves if needed. Spread the egg mixture across the lettuce, dividing it evenly among the 4 slices. Using a sharp knife, cut each piece of bread twice on a diagonal to make 4 triangles.

Sprinkle each with a few of the onion sprouts and flower petals. *Makes 16 open-face tea sandwiches*

Seafood and Saffron Quiche

QUICHES ARE FRENCH-STYLE CUSTARDS BAKED IN A CRUST. SAFFRON LENDS A HAUNTING FLAVOR AND A LOVELY GOLD COLOR.

PASTRY DOUGH

2 cups all-purpose flour

1 teaspoon salt

1/2 cup (1 stick) cold, unsalted butter, cut into small pieces

6 tablespoons ice water

FILLING

3 tablespoons dry white wine

1/4 teaspoon saffron threads

6 tablespoons butter

1/4 cup minced green onions, including
some of the green

2 ounces shrimp, peeled, deveined, and chopped

6 ounces fresh lump crabmeat, shredded

1/2 teaspoon salt

1/2 teaspoon freshly ground pepper

3 eggs

1 cup heavy cream

1 tablespoon tomato paste

1/8 teaspoon cayenne pepper

1/4 cup shredded Swiss cheese

To make the pastry: Preheat the oven to 400°F. Sift the flour and salt together into a bowl. With a pastry blender, cut the butter into the flour mixture until pea-sized balls form. Using a fork, stir in the ice water 1 tablespoon at a time. Gather the dough into a ball, wrap it in plastic, and refrigerate for 15 minutes.

On a lightly floured surface, roll the dough out into 1/8-inch-thick circle. Drape the dough over the rolling pin and unfold it over a 10-inch round quiche or tart pan, pressing it gently into the pan. Trim off the excess dough level with the pan. Line the pastry shell with aluminum foil. Add a layer of pastry weights or dried beans, and bake for 7 to 8 minutes. Remove it from the oven and lift out the foil and weights. Prick the bottom with a fork and return the shell to the oven, baking another 4 to 5 minutes, or until slightly firm. Remove the shell and let cool completely before filling.

To make the filling: In a small saucepan, heat the wine and saffron until it boils. Remove from heat. Let stand for 20 minutes.

In a medium skillet, melt 3 tablespoons of butter over medium heat. Add the onions and sauté them for 1 minute, or just until limp. Add the seafood, salt, and pepper, cook for 1 to 2 minutes, then add the wine mixture. Remove from heat and let cool.

Lower the oven temperature to 375°F. In a medium bowl, beat together the eggs, cream, tomato paste, and cayenne pepper until blended. Stir in the shellfish mixture. Put the pastry shell on a baking sheet and pour in the egg mixture. Sprinkle with cheese, dot with the remaining butter and bake for 30 minutes, or until a knife inserted into the center comes out clean. Cool for at least 10 to 15 minutes before serving. *Serves 4 to 6*

Roasted Tomatoes Filled with Herbed Eggs

THE TART, SWEET TASTE OF ROASTED TOMATOES, AN ENGLISH SPECIALTY, IS A PERFECT BACKGROUND

FOR BASIL-FLECKED SCRAMBLED EGGS. SERVE THESE AS A MAIN COURSE FOR BREAKFAST, BRUNCH, OR SUPPER,

OR AS AN ACCOMPANIMENT TO SMOKED SALMON, GRILLED HAM STEAK, OR BACON.

4 ripe but firm tomatoes

Extra-virgin olive oil

1 teaspoon salt

1 teaspoon freshly ground pepper

8 eggs

2 tablespoons unsalted butter

2 tablespoons chopped fresh basil,
plus 8 small basil leaves or
sprigs for garnish

Preheat the oven to 400°F. With a sharp knife, cut the upper one-third from each of the tomatoes and discard. With a metal spoon, scoop out the pulp and seeds, leaving the outer shell. (Save the tomato parts for soup.) Sprinkle the inside of each tomato cavity with a little olive oil. Season all the cavities with 1/2 teaspoon of the salt and 1/2 teaspoon of the pepper. Place the tomato shells in a small, shallow baking dish and bake for 10 to 12 minutes, or until the tomatoes just begin to change color.

While the tomatoes are roasting, cook the eggs. In a medium bowl, beat the eggs with the remaining 1/2 teaspoon salt and 1/2 teaspoon pepper until just blended. In a medium skillet, melt the butter over medium heat. When the butter foams, pour in the eggs. Reduce heat to low and cook, stirring frequently, until cooked to nearly the desired consistency, about 5 to 6 minutes for a soft curd, 7 to 8 for a firmer one. Stir in the chopped basil and cook for 1 minute.

Fill the roasted tomatoes to heaping with the eggs. Garnish each with a basil leaf or sprig and serve hot. *Serves 4*

Wild Mushroom Crepes

TRADITIONAL FRENCH EGG-BATTER CREPES ARE EASY TO MAKE AND CAN BE SERVED IN A VARIETY OF WAYS.

FILLING

4 tablespoons unsalted butter

2 shallots, minced

6 ounces chanterelle mushrooms, chopped

4 ounces wood ear mushrooms, chopped

6 ounces shiitake mushrooms, chopped

4 ounces white button mushrooms, chopped

1/2 teaspoon salt

1/2 teaspoon freshly ground pepper

1/2 to 2/3 cup dry white wine

2 tablespoons minced fresh parsley

2 teaspoons minced fresh thyme leaves

5 ounces crumbled fresh white goat cheese

3/4 cup (3 ounces) shredded Swiss cheese

CREPES

4 eggs

1-3/4 cups milk

1/3 cup all-purpose flour

1/8 teaspoon salt

7 tablespoons unsalted butter

To make the filling: In a large skillet, melt the butter over medium heat. Add the shallots and sauté 2 minutes until translucent. Add all the mushrooms and sauté for 3 to 4 minutes. Sprinkle with salt and pepper and stir. Using a slotted spoon, remove the mushrooms to a plate. Increase heat to high and add the wine and stir. Cook to reduce the liquid in the skillet by half. Remove from heat and stir in the parsley, thyme, and goat cheese. Set aside.

To make the crepe batter: In a large bowl, whisk together the eggs and milk. Gradually whisk in the flour and salt to make a thin, lump-free batter. Cover and refrigerate for 2 hours. The batter should be the consistency of thick cream.

Heat an 8-inch crepe pan or skillet and melt 1 teaspoon of the butter, coating the pan by tipping it from side to side. Pour a scant 1/4 cup batter into the pan, quickly tipping and turning the pan to coat the bottom. When the batter begins to bubble on its surface and the edges pull away from the pan, turn over the crepe and cook it just a moment. Remove to a plate and keep warm. Repeat until all the batter has been used.

Butter an 8-by-12-inch baking dish. Spoon 1 tablespoon filling in a line down the center of each crepe. Roll the crepes, then place them seam-side down in the baking dish. Pour the filling juices over the crepes, dot with 1 tablespoon butter, and sprinkle with Swiss cheese. Bake for 15 minutes, then place under a broiler just long enough to brown the surface. Serve immediately.

Makes 16 crepes. Serves 8 as a first course, 4 as a main course

Beef- and Egg-Filled Piroshki in a Puff-Pastry Crust

HARD-BOILED EGGS ARE AN IMPORTANT INGREDIENT IN THE FILLING OF PIROSHKI
AND ARE SOMETIMES THE MAIN COMPONENT. THE LITTLE PIES MAKE A DELICIOUS APPETIZER OR AN ACCOMPANIMENT
TO A HEARTY SOUP SUCH AS BORSCHT, ANOTHER RUSSIAN CLASSIC.

1 teaspoon unsalted butter

1 small onion, finely chopped

8 ounces extra-lean ground beef, crumbled

1/4 cup beef broth

2 hard-boiled eggs, chopped

1/2 teaspoon salt

1/2 teaspoon freshly ground pepper

1 tablespoon minced fresh dill

2 sheets frozen puff pastry, thawed

1 egg, lightly beaten

Preheat the oven to 375°F. In a large skillet, heat the butter over medium heat. When it foams, add the onion and sauté for 2 to 3 minutes, or until translucent. Add the beef and cook, stirring, until it is lightly browned, about 4 to 5 minutes. Add the broth, eggs, salt, pepper, and dill, and cook for 1 to 2 minutes, stirring. Remove from heat and let cool to room temperature.

On a lightly floured board, roll out the puff pastry dough into a 1/4-inch-thick sheet. Using a biscuit cutter, cut out 4-inch circles. Place 1 tablespoon filling in the center of each circle. Using a small pastry or paint brush, brush a little beaten egg along the edges. Fold over, making a half circle, and pinch the edges together to seal. Set aside. Repeat until all the filling is used.

Brush the top of each piroshki with some of the remaining beaten egg. Place on a baking sheet and bake for about 30 minutes, or until golden. *Makes 30 to 35 pies; serves 8 to 12 as appetizers*

Old-Fashioned Custard Pie

THIS IS ONE OF THE CLASSICS OF ENGLISH AND AMERICAN COOKING. ITS LIGHT FLAVOR AND DELICATE TEXTURE
MAKE A DELIGHTFUL FINISH TO ANY MEAL.

Pastry Dough (see page 77)

FILLING

3 cups milk

3 eggs, lightly beaten

1/2 cup granulated sugar

1/4 teaspoon salt

1/2 teaspoon vanilla extract

1/4 teaspoon freshly grated nutmeg

Preheat the oven to 425°F. Prepare the dough and refrigerate it for 15 minutes.

On a lightly floured surface, roll the dough out into a 1/8-inch-thick circle. Drape the dough over the rolling pin and rest it over a 9-inch pie pan. Unfold the dough and press it gently into the pan. Trim the dough to a 1/2-inch overhang, fold it under the rim, and crimp it with the tips of your fingers to make a decorative edge on the crust.

To make the filling: In a medium saucepan, heat the milk over medium-high heat just until bubbles form around the edge. Remove and set aside. In a medium bowl, beat together the eggs, sugar, salt, vanilla, and nutmeg just until blended. Gradually stir in the hot milk. Immediately pour the egg mixture into the pastry-lined pan.

Bake for 15 minutes, or until the edges of the crust are browned. Reduce the heat to 300°F and bake 35 to 40 minutes, or until all but the very center, an area about the size of a nickel, is set. Test this by gently shaking the pie. Remove from the oven and set aside on a wire rack to cool for at least 1 hour. Serve warm, at room temperature, or chilled. *Serves 6*

Pôts de Crème

PÔTS DE CRÈME ARE DELICATE FRENCH CUSTARDS USUALLY MADE AND PRESENTED IN SPECIAL CUPS USED JUST FOR THAT PURPOSE, ALTHOUGH PYREX CUSTARD CUPS WILL DO INSTEAD. THE CUSTARDS CAN BE DRESSED UP WITH FRUIT SAUCES OR A BIT OF WHIPPED CREAM AND SHAVED CHOCOLATE.

2 eggs

4 tablespoons granulated sugar

1-1/2 cups milk

1/2 teaspoon vanilla extract

Preheat the oven to 350°F. Butter four 6-ounce ramekins or custard cups. Sprinkle each with sugar, then shake out any excess.

In a medium bowl, beat together the eggs and sugar until pale yellow and thick enough to form a slowly dissolving ribbon on the surface when the whisk or beater is lifted. In a small saucepan, heat the milk until it steams; do not boil it. Gradually whisk the milk and vanilla into the egg mixture. Strain the mixture through a fine-meshed sieve into a clean bowl or large measuring cup with a pouring spout.

Divide the mixture among the prepared ramekins. Place them in a baking dish and pour boiling water into the dish until it reaches halfway up the sides of the ramekins. Place the dish in the oven and bake for 40 to 50 minutes, or until a knife inserted in the center comes out clean.

Remove the cups from the water bath and set aside to cool slightly. Serve warm, at room temperature, or chilled.
Serves 4

Spanish Flan

A CREAMY, CARAMEL-TOPPED CUSTARD, FLAN IS A CLASSIC DESSERT IN BOTH SPAIN AND FRANCE, WHERE IT OFTEN ENDS

THE MEAL. FOR A VARIATION, ADD A LITTLE BRANDY, RUM, OR COGNAC TO THE HOT MILK MIXTURE BEFORE BAKING.

1-1/4 cups granulated sugar

2 cups milk

2 cups half-and-half

6 eggs

1/2 teaspoon salt

2 teaspoons vanilla extract

Preheat the oven to 325°F. Place an 8-1/2-by-1-1/2-inch round Pyrex pie dish in the oven to warm.

In a large, heavy skillet, heat 3/4 cup of the sugar over medium-high heat. Stir as the sugar melts to form a light-brown syrup. Immediately pour the syrup into the heated pie dish. Holding the dish with pot holders, tip it so the syrup covers the bottom and the sides. Set aside.

In a medium saucepan, heat the milk and half-and-half over medium heat just until bubbles form around the edge. Break the eggs into a large bowl and beat them with a whisk until just blended. Stir in the remaining 1/2 cup sugar, salt, and vanilla. Gradually stir in the hot milk mixture.

Set the pie dish in a shallow pan and pour the milk mixture into the dish. Pour boiling water in the shallow pan to reach halfway up the sides of the baking dish.

Place in the oven and bake for 35 to 40 minutes, or until a knife inserted into the center comes out clean. Remove and let cool to room temperature. Refrigerate at least 4 hours before serving, or overnight.

To serve, run a knife around the edge of the dish to loosen the custard. Invert a serving plate on top of the dish, and holding the dish and plate firmly, turn them over, unmolding the flan onto the plate. Pour any remaining caramel over the flan if desired. Cut into wedges to serve. *Serves 8*

decorative eggs

7

Eggshell Candles

THIS IS AN UNCOMPLICATED WAY TO MAKE FESTIVE, SEASONAL CANDLES.

YOU WILL NEED:

Egg cutter or sharp knife

Raw eggs

Clear candle wax (sold in
large blocks at craft stores)

Meat or candy thermometer

Colored wax chips (available
at craft stores)

Wire-centered wicks and
metal wick holders (available at
craft stores)

Empty egg carton

Water-based acrylic paints

Decorative plate and rocks,
sand-filled votives,
or egg cups

TO MAKE:

Use the egg cutter or knife to crack off one-third of the shell at the narrow end of each egg. Empty out the white and yolk, and gently rinse and dry the shell.

In a double boiler, or in a coffee can set in a saucepan of water, melt the clear wax to 160°F, testing with the thermometer. Reduce heat, add the wax chips, and heat until the chips melt.

Cut a piece of wick about 6 inches long for each egg and put a wick holder on one end.

Set the eggshells in the egg carton and fill each one about one-third full with wax. Put a wick and wick holder into the bottom center of each shell and let the wax dry, about 10 minutes.

Fill the eggshells 1/4 inch from the top with wax and let harden completely, about 1 hour.

Paint the eggshells the desired color and let dry.

Place the eggshell candles in a plate of rocks, in sand-filled votives, or in egg cups.

Egg Gift Boxes

THIS IS A STYLISH ADORNMENT FOR BABY GIFTS OR BABY-SHOWER GIFTS FOR MOTHERS-TO-BE.

YOU WILL NEED:

Gift boxes with gifts, plus small empty gift box

Easter grass, colored or clear

Dyed empty eggs

Tape

Hot-glue gun and glue sticks (optional)

Ribbon

Baby rattle (optional)

TO MAKE:

Stack the gift boxes by size with the empty one on top, placed open-end up in its lid. Fill the top box with Easter grass and place an egg in it. Secure the stack of boxes with tape or glue if necessary between each tier. Tie the ribbon firmly around the stack and over the egg.

OPTION

Tie the ribbon around a single gift box and make a large bow on top, securing the baby rattle. Hot glue an eggshell to the bow or box top.

Easter-Egg Cookie Tree

A COOKIE TREE MADE WITH FLOWERING
SPRING BRANCHES IS A LOVELY DECORATION FOR
THE HOME AT EASTERTIME. AT ANY HOLIDAY
GATHERING THAT INCLUDES CHILDREN, IT WILL
SURELY BE THE CENTER OF ATTENTION.

YOU WILL NEED:

Floral foam blocks

Sharp knife

Watering can

Heavy-stemmed flowering tree branches such as dogwood, cherry, plum, or almond

Easter Egg Cookies (page 28)

Narrow ribbon

Scissors

TO MAKE:

Soak the floral foam in water until it is full. Trim it to fit with the knife, then put it inside the watering can partially filled with water.

Poke the lower end of the branches into the floral foam. String the cookies with pieces of the ribbon cut with scissors and tie the ribbons to the branches.

Ukrainian Eggs

KNOWN AS *PYSANKY*, THESE EGGS ARE A TRADITIONAL ART THAT IS OVER A THOUSAND YEARS OLD. THE CONTENTS OF THE EGGS WILL DRY OUT VERY SLOWLY, AND THE VARNISHED EGGS WILL LAST FOR YEARS.

YOU WILL NEED:

Raw eggs at room temperature

Ukrainian egg decorating kit

OR

Pencil without eraser

Kistka with medium tip
(Ukrainian wax writing instrument,
available at craft stores)

Candle

Cake of pure beeswax

Egg dyes in light and dark colors,
hot water, distilled white vinegar

Small dishes or cups

Egg rack made by thrusting 3 nails
up through an egg carton so the points
form a small triangle

Spoons

Tissues

Wax remover (turpentine or De-solv-it)

A small brush and Spar varnish

TO MAKE:

Use the pencil to mark each egg in equal sections. Do not erase—it will cause smudging. Holding an egg in one hand, draw a line from the top to the bottom of the egg on each side by rotating the egg against the pencil. Starting at the middle of the egg, draw another line around the circumference, marking the egg into quarters. Starting where the two lines cross, draw diagonals around the egg in each quarter, ending where the 2 lines cross on the other side.

Heat the kistka over the candle. When hot, sink its head into the beeswax, drawing a small amount of beeswax into the core. With the kistka, trace the pencil lines, covering them with wax.

Prepare the egg dyes. Working from lightest to darkest colors, put the egg in a light color dye until it attains the desired hue (5 to 10 minutes). Remove to the rack with spoons and let dry.

With the kistka, make additional lines and designs as desired. Dip the egg in the next color dye. Remove to the rack and let dry. Repeat this step as many times as desired, leaving the egg in the last dye color until it becomes quite dark (15 to 20 minutes). Remove to the rack and let dry.

Slowly move the egg back and forth at the side of the candle flame to melt the wax. Remove the soft wax with a tissue. Use a small amount of wax remover on a tissue to finish cleaning the egg. The shell must be completely free of wax before varnishing.

With the brush, apply a thin coat of varnish and let dry, which may take up to several hours.

Experiment with other designs, kistka tip sizes, and color sequences.

airy eggs

Oeufs à la Neige

OEUFS À LA NEIGE, OR "EGGS IN THE SNOW," IS A CLASSIC FRENCH DESSERT OF
POACHED SOFT MERINGUE PUFFS FLOATING ON A POOL OF CRÈME ANGLAISE. TOP THEM WITH SLICED STRAWBERRIES
FOR A BEAUTIFUL ENDING TO A SPECIAL SPRING MEAL LIKE A MOTHER'S DAY LUNCH.

MERINGUES

6 egg whites

3/4 cup granulated sugar

1/4 teaspoon salt

1/4 teaspoon vanilla extract

4 cups milk

CRÈME ANGLAISE

2 cups milk, reserved from meringues above

2 egg yolks

2 eggs

1/4 cup granulated sugar

1/8 teaspoon salt

1 teaspoon vanilla extract

4 cups fresh strawberries, hulled and sliced

To make the meringues: In a large bowl, beat the egg whites until soft peaks form. Gradually add the sugar, salt, and vanilla, beating until the whites form stiff, glossy peaks.

In a large, heavy skillet, heat the milk over medium heat just until tiny bubbles form around the edge. Reduce heat to low.

Spoon 2 or 3 mounds of egg whites, about 1/4 heaping cupful each, onto the hot milk, spacing them 1 inch or so apart. Cook over medium heat for 3 minutes, or just until firm. Using a slotted spoon, turn the mounds and cook another 2 to 3 minutes. Transfer to paper towels to drain. Repeat to use the remaining mixture, making 16 meringues. Transfer the puffs to a large plate lined with clean paper towels. Cover loosely with plastic wrap and chill for several hours, or overnight.

To make the crème anglaise: In a double boiler, heat the milk to just below boiling. In a medium bowl, beat the yolks and the eggs together until just blended, then add the sugar, salt, and vanilla, and gradually stir in the hot milk. Return the mixture to the double boiler and cook over boiling water until the mixture thickens enough to coat the back of a spoon. Remove from heat immediately. Let cool slightly to thicken.

To serve, pour about 1/3 cup crème anglaise into each of 8 shallow dessert bowls or dishes, top each with 2 chilled meringues, and sprinkle with some of the strawberries. *Serves 8*

Raspberry Sabayon

SABAYON IN FRENCH, OR *ZABAGLIONE* IN ITALIAN, IS A FROTHY CUSTARD FLAVORED
WITH MARSALA OR SHERRY AND SOMETIMES LIGHTENED WITH EGG WHITES. DEPENDING ON THE SEASON,
FRUITS ARE SOMETIMES INCORPORATED AS WELL. IT MAKES AN ELEGANT HOLIDAY DESSERT,
ESPECIALLY WHEN SERVED IN SPARKLING CRYSTAL.

3 eggs, separated

2 tablespoons Marsala or dry sherry

4 tablespoons granulated sugar

1/4 teaspoon gelatin dissolved in
2 tablespoons warm water

2 cups fresh raspberries

In a double boiler, mix together the egg yolks, Marsala, and 3 tablespoons of the sugar. Cook over barely simmering water, stirring constantly, until a thick custard forms, about 5 to 7 minutes. The custard should be thick enough to coat the back of a metal spoon and to leave a path when you draw the spoon through it. Stir in the gelatin mixture. Remove from heat and set aside to cool.

In a medium bowl, combine all but 1/3 cup of the raspberries with the remaining 1 tablespoon sugar and mash them together to make a puree. Set aside.

In a large bowl, beat the egg whites until stiff peaks form. Fold the egg whites into the cooled custard, then fold in the crushed raspberries. Spoon into a serving bowl. Refrigerate at least 2 hours. To serve, garnish with the remaining raspberries. *Serves 4*

Salzburger Nockerln

THESE INCREDIBLY LIGHT AND DELICIOUS DUMPLINGS, WHICH ARE REALLY SOUFFLÉS,
WERE FIRST MADE IN THE 1600S TO BE SERVED AT THE TABLE OF THE ARCHBISHOP OF SALZBURG, AND THEY REMAIN
AN AUSTRIAN FAVORITE TODAY. THEY MAKE AN IMPRESSIVE ENTRANCE WORTHY OF ANY HOLIDAY CELEBRATION.

1/2 cup (1 stick) unsalted butter at room temperature

1/4 cup granulated sugar

4 eggs, separated

1/4 cup all-purpose flour

1/2 cup milk

2 tablespoons vanilla sugar or regular granulated sugar

Preheat the oven to 425°F. In a large bowl, cream the butter until pale in color. Add the sugar and continue beating until fluffy. Add the egg yolks, one at a time, beating until they are thoroughly mixed into the butter mixture. In a large bowl, beat the egg whites until stiff peaks form. Using a spatula, fold the whites into the butter mixture in two portions, alternating with the flour.

Pour the milk into a large ovenproof skillet or flame-proof baking dish and bring it to a boil. Carefully pour the egg and butter mixture over the milk, spreading it to cover the milk evenly. Immediately put the pan or dish into the oven and bake until the dumpling is golden brown and the milk has been absorbed, 3 to 4 minutes.

Remove from the oven and scoop out large portions of the dumpling onto 4 dessert plates. Sprinkle with the vanilla sugar and serve immediately. *Serves 4*

Cheese Soufflé

A CHEESE SOUFFLÉ, A GREEN SALAD, AND STEAMED ASPARAGUS ARE
THE QUINTESSENTIAL EASTER BRUNCH, BUT CONSIDER THIS SOUFFLÉ FOR DINNER AS WELL,
AS AN ACCOMPANIMENT TO A ROAST LEG OF LAMB OR AN EASTER HAM.

1/4 cup grated Parmesan cheese

4 eggs, separated

1 egg white

2-1/2 tablespoons unsalted butter

2 tablespoons minced shallots

3 tablespoons all-purpose flour

1/2 teaspoon salt

1 teaspoon freshly ground pepper

1 cup milk

1/4 cup shredded Swiss cheese

Preheat the oven to 400°F. Butter a 3-cup soufflé mold. Sprinkle the mold with half the Parmesan cheese, shaking the mold to coat the inside with the cheese.

In a large bowl, beat the 5 egg whites until stiff, glossy peaks form. In a medium bowl, beat the egg yolks until they are well blended.

In a large, heavy saucepan, melt the butter over medium heat. Add the shallots and sauté until translucent, 2 to 3 minutes. Remove the pan from heat and whisk in the flour, salt, and pepper until a paste forms. Return the pan to medium heat and gradually whisk in the milk in a steady stream. Reduce heat to low and stir until there are no lumps. Simmer the sauce, stirring occasionally, until it is thick enough to coat a spoon, about 10 minutes.

Remove the pan from heat and whisk in the egg yolks until the mixture is smooth and creamy. Whisk in the Swiss cheese and all but 1 teaspoon of the remaining Parmesan cheese, whisking until the cheese has melted. Remove from heat and let cool for a few minutes. Stir one-fourth of the beaten egg whites into the egg yolk mixture, then carefully fold in the remaining egg whites.

Spoon the soufflé mixture into the prepared mold, filling it three-fourths full. Sprinkle with the remaining Parmesan cheese. Bake for 5 minutes, then reduce the temperature to 375°F. Bake until the soufflé is puffy and golden brown and a knife or a wooden skewer inserted into the center comes out clean, about 25 minutes. Serve immediately, scooping out portions with a serving spoon. *Serves 4 to 6*

Individual Orange Soufflés

INDIVIDUAL SOUFFLÉS BAKED IN HOLLOWED-OUT ORANGES ARE AN INTRIGUING HOLIDAY PRESENTATION THAT FASCINATES CHILDREN, WHILE THEIR FEATHER-LIGHT TEXTURE AND INTENSE ORANGE FLAVOR DELIGHTS EVERYONE.

6 navel oranges

1 tablespoon unsalted butter

1 tablespoon all-purpose flour

1/3 cup granulated sugar

1/4 teaspoon salt

4 eggs, separated

Preheat an oven to 325°F. Cut off the top third of each orange and reserve the tops. Using a large metal spoon, scoop out the oranges, putting the pulp of 4 oranges into a bowl and saving the rest for another use. In a blender, process the pulp until just pureed, 45 seconds to 1 minute. Pour the pulp through a sieve into a medium bowl, pressing on it gently with the back of a wooden spoon to release the juice. Using a zester or peeler, remove the zest from the reserved orange tops. Mince the zest and reserve 1 tablespoon.

In a large saucepan, combine the juice and butter. Bring to a boil and continue to boil for 3 to 4 minutes, until reduced by one-fourth. Stir in the minced zest. Reduce heat to low and whisk in the flour to make a smooth paste. Whisk in the sugar and salt and cook, stirring constantly, for 3 to 4 minutes, until the mixture thickens and becomes gel-like.

Remove from heat and gradually whisk in the egg yolks until a creamy mixture forms and the color lightens, 1 to 2 minutes.

In a large bowl, beat the egg whites until stiff, glossy peaks form. Fold the egg whites into the juice mixture. Fill the 6 orange shells equally with the mixture. Place the shells on a baking sheet and bake for 15 to 18 minutes, or until the soufflés are puffed and lightly golden. Serve immediately.

Serves 6

Meringues with Blackberries

THESE MERINGUES ARE CRISP, CRUNCHY VERSIONS OF THE MERINGUE TOPPING FOUND ON PIES.

AS THEY SLOWLY BAKE AT A LOW TEMPERATURE, THE MOISTURE EVAPORATES, LEAVING BEHIND A DELICATE, LIGHT SHELL.

IN FRANCE, THESE ARE COMMONLY USED AS A BASE FOR FRUITS AND ICE CREAMS. THE SHELLS ARE

WHITE BUT CAN EASILY BE TINTED USING A DROP OR TWO OF FOOD COLORING. FOR AN ESPECIALLY FESTIVE FINALE,

TOP THE MERINGUES WITH A SCOOP OF ICE CREAM BEFORE ADDING THE BLACKBERRIES.

6 egg whites

1/8 teaspoon salt

1-1/2 teaspoons cream of tartar
(omit if using a copper bowl)

1 teaspoon vanilla extract

1-1/2 cups plus 2 tablespoons granulated sugar

4 cups fresh blackberries

Preheat the oven to 250°F. In a large bowl, beat the egg whites with the salt and cream of tartar until soft peaks form. Add the vanilla extract. Gradually add the 1-1/2 cups sugar a few tablespoons at a time, beating after each addition until stiff, glossy peaks form.

To make the shells: Line a baking sheet with a piece of ungreased brown paper, such as a piece cut from a paper grocery bag, or parchment paper. Scoop up about 3/4 of a cup of the mixture and drop it onto the paper into a mound about 3 inches in diameter. With the back of a spoon, shape a shallow well in the center of the mound. Repeat to use the remaining meringue.

Bake the meringues for 1 hour. Turn off the heat and let the meringues cool in the oven at least 2 hours or overnight, if possible. Slip the meringues into a paper bag in a single layer, fold the top over, and store them in a dry place until ready to use, up to 3 or 4 days.

To make the filling: In a medium bowl, combine the blackberries with the 2 tablespoons sugar. With the back of a spoon, mash some of the blackberries. Cover and refrigerate for several hours.

To serve, place the meringues on individual dessert plates and spoon some of the blackberries and their juice over each. *Makes 8 to 10 shells; serves 8 to 10*

Index

List of Recipes

List of Crafts